8/01

REVOLUTIONARY WAR

To celebrate the signing of the Declaration of Independence, colonial soldiers in New York gleefully topple a statue of Great Britain's King George III.

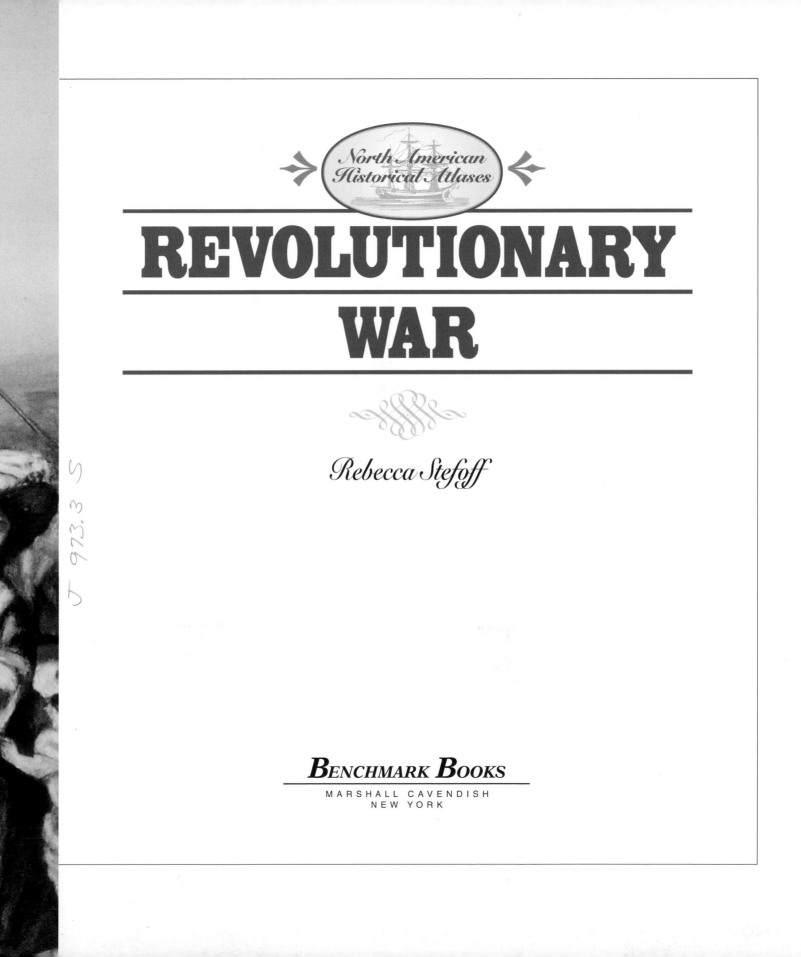

North American Historical Atlases

REVOLUTIONARY WAR

Rebecca Stefoff

BENCHMARK BOOKS

MARSHALL CAVENDISH
NEW YORK

Benchmark Books
Marshall Cavendish Corporation
99 White Plains Road
Tarrytown, New York 10591

• • •

Library of Congress Cataloging-in-Publication Data
Stefoff, Rebecca, date.
Revolutionary War/Rebecca Stefoff
p. cm—(North American Historical Atlases)
Includes bibliographical references (p.) and index.
Summary: Examines the causes, events, and aftermath of America's war for independence.
ISBN 0-7614-1058-9 (lib.bdg.)
1. United States—History—Revolution, 1775–1783—Juvenile literature.   2. United States—History—Revolution,
1775–1783—Maps—Juvenile literature.   [1. United States—History—Revolution, 1775–1783.]   I. Title.
E208 .S83   2001   99-047937   973.3—dc21

• • •

Printed in Hong Kong
1 3 5 7 8 6 4 2

• • •

Book Designer: Judith Turziano
Photo Researcher: Matthew Dudley

• • •

CREDITS
Front cover: *Corbis-Bettmann*—Map illustrating the Battle of Long Island, August 27, 1776.
Back cover: *Giraudon/Art Resource*—Painting by Couder, Louis Charles Auguste. Siege of Yorktown, 1781.

The photographs and maps in this book are used by permission and through
the courtesy of: *Corbis-Bettmann*: 2–3, 7,10, 13, 16, 18, 19, 21, 25, 27, 32, 35, 36, 40, 43.
The Library of Congress Maps Division: 11, 14, 17, 24, 29, 31, 33, 38, 40.

Contents

Chapter One

THE ROAD TO WAR

For most of the 1700s the British and the French fought over eastern North America like two dogs battling over a bone. Finally the British won that fight, but then something else went wrong. The bone started biting back.

North America in 1763

The war that broke out between Great Britain and France in 1754 came to be called the Seven Years' War in Europe. But this war was also fought in North America's **frontier** settlements and trackless forests. The British colonists and soldiers there called it the French and Indian War because it pitted them against two enemies, the French in Canada and the Native Americans, known as Indians, who sided with them.

Indians fought on the British side, too, but not as many of them. The Native Americans believed the British were more likely than the French to take their land away from them—and they were right. The British had already settled the whole Atlantic coast, pushing the Indians aside. By 1753 some British-American colonists were making plans to move west into the Ohio River valley. One of them, a twenty-one-year-old Virginian named George Washington, went into the Ohio country to warn the French out of the area. The French scornfully turned him away.

War began the next year. Seven years later France had lost more than its dream of con-trolling the Ohio and Mississippi valleys. It had also lost Canada, which now belonged to the British. And, in addition to its original thirteen colonies and Canada, Britain now controlled the huge, mostly unexplored territory between the Appalachian Mountains and the Mississippi River—a territory that included the Ohio River valley. Far in the west, beyond the Mississippi River, was the Louisiana Territory, now owned by Spain. But in 1763 the colonists of British North America were not looking that far west. They had enough problems closer to home.

British North America

By the 1760s more than two million people lived in the thirteen colonies of British North America. However, they did not think of themselves as sharing an "American" identity. There was little unity among the colonies. Each had its own relationship with Great Britain, its own form of local government, and its own distinctive history. The ethnic background and religious practices of the colonists varied considerably from colony to colony. So did economic life. Some colonies allowed slavery, and some did not. The northern colonies thrived on trade, shipping, and the beginnings of industry, while the southern economy was based on **plantation agriculture**.

The thirteen colonies were Massachusetts (which included what is now Maine), New Hampshire, New York, Rhode Island, Con-

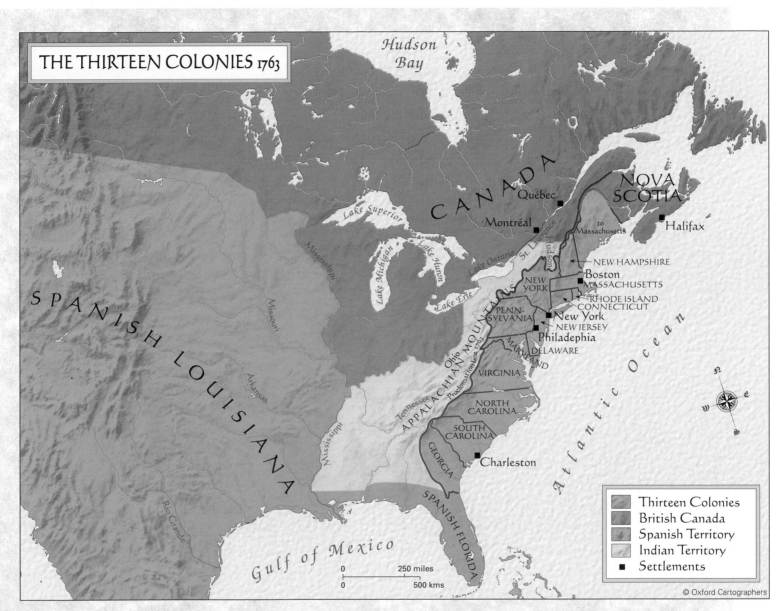

THE THIRTEEN COLONIES 1763

Hudson Bay

CANADA

NOVA SCOTIA

Québec

Montréal

to Massachusetts

Halifax

Lake Superior

Lake Michigan

Lake Huron

Lake Ontario

Lake Erie

St. Lawrence

Hudson

NEW HAMPSHIRE

NEW YORK

Boston

MASSACHUSETTS

RHODE ISLAND

CONNECTICUT

New York

NEW JERSEY

PENN-SYLVANIA

Philadephia

DELAWARE

MARYLAND

VIRGINIA

Ohio

APPALACHIAN MOUNTAINS

Proclamation line 1763

Tennessee

NORTH CAROLINA

SOUTH CAROLINA

GEORGIA

Charleston

Mississippi

Missouri

Arkansas

SPANISH LOUISIANA

Rio Grande

Gulf of Mexico

SPANISH FLORIDA

Atlantic Ocean

	Thirteen Colonies
	British Canada
	Spanish Territory
	Indian Territory
■	Settlements

0   250 miles
0   500 kms

In 1763, at the end of the French and Indian War and on the eve of the American Revolution, two powers controlled North America. The west and Florida belonged to Spain, while Great Britain had Canada and the thirteen Atlantic colonies. British settlers had already begun crowding into the central territory set aside for the Indians.

HUNGRY FOR LAND

 When the French and Indian War ended, some colonists were packed and ready to push westward across the Appalachian Mountains to new frontiers. They had even formed companies to buy and sell land west of the mountains—George Washington was a member of one such company. But those who thought the British victory had cleared the way for them to settle the Ohio River valley got a nasty shock. To prevent war with the Native Americans of the Ohio country, the British government declared that the land west of the Appalachian Mountains would remain Indian country. Colonists were forbidden to cross the Appalachians. This law, called the Proclamation of 1763, disappointed and angered colonists who felt they had fought the French and Indian War to open up the Ohio country for settlers. It was just one of many things that turned American colonists against Britain in the late 1700s.

claims. One of the biggest struggles of the coming Revolutionary War would be getting people from all the colonies to work together for a common goal—and to think of themselves as Americans, not Virginians, Bostonians, or New Yorkers.

Unpopular Laws

The Seven Years' War had cost Great Britain a lot of money. To get some of it back, Britain announced that the American colonists would have to pay new taxes. Many colonists were outraged. The New York colonial legislature thun-

The Stamp Act of 1765 forced colonists in America to pay for stamps like these on newspapers, books, playing cards, advertisements, legal documents, and other printed items. Printers and lawyers, who had much influence in colonial society, led American protests against the Stamp Act.

necticut, New Jersey, Pennsylvania, Delaware, Maryland, Virginia, North Carolina, South Carolina, and Georgia. They were so far from being unified that they often quarreled with one another, usually over boundaries and land

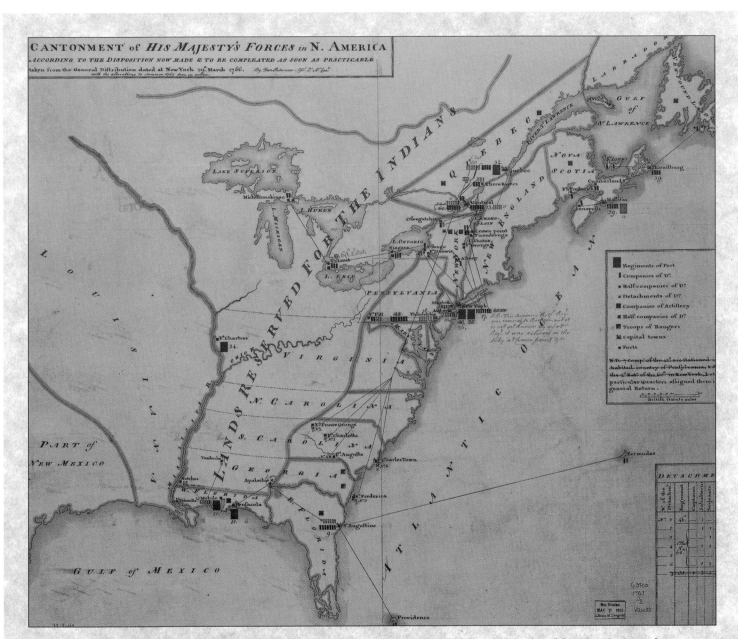

A 1766 British Army map shows how many troops Great Britain maintained in North America and where they were stationed. Note the forces in Florida, which belonged to Spain for most of the colonial period but fell under British control for twenty years before Spain got it back in 1783.

CAUSE OF CONFLICT
BETWEEN GREAT BRITAIN AND AMERICA

YEAR	ACT	EFFECTS
1650–1696	Navigation Acts	Limited colonial trade to British-owned ships.
1699	Woolen Act	Prevented the colonists from selling wool or woolen products to other countries.
1733	Molasses Act	Set high taxes on imported sugar, molasses, and rum.
1750	Iron Act	Forbade the colonists to build new iron-working plants; aimed at forcing them to buy iron from British manufacturers at prices favorable to the British.
1764	Sugar Act	Attempted to end the smuggling of West Indian molasses by the colonists; set up special British-controlled courts to try smuggling cases.
1765	Stamp Act	Placed a tax on almost all printed material.
1765	Quartering Act	Required colonists to help pay the cost of housing British troops.
1767	Townshend Duties	Placed new import taxes on such goods as paper, glass, china, and paint.
1774	Coercive Acts	Punished colonists for Boston Tea Party by closing Boston Harbor; outlawed town meetings; forced colonists to house British troops in their homes; called the Intolerable Acts by colonists.

dered, "There can be no liberty, no happiness, no security" while the British treasury grew rich at the expense of colonial taxpayers.

The Stamp Act of 1765 was one of the most hated new laws. It required colonists to pay a British official to stamp almost every printed item. After widespread protests the British government canceled the Stamp Act, but in 1767 it passed new laws called the Townshend Acts that raised the price of imported goods such as glass, paper, and tea. Soon colonists hated the Townshend Acts even more than the Stamp Act.

Great Britain never made as much money as it had hoped from these taxes. Instead, the laws backfired against Britain by convincing many American colonists that the British government was treating them unfairly. At protests and demonstrations colonists cried, "No taxation without representation." They did not want to pay British taxes as long as they were not given a voice in the British government.

Hotbed of Rebellion

Outrage against Britain's new policies was especially strong in Boston, Massachusetts. Britain sent 700 red-coated soldiers there to keep order, but fights between the colonists and the redcoats were not uncommon. In March of 1770 one scuffle turned ugly when soldiers fired on a rioting mob. Five colonists were killed in what came to be called the Boston Massacre.

Three years later, to protest a tax on tea, Bostonians, led by Samuel Adams, threw a shipload of tea into the harbor. They disguised themselves as Indians, but their disguises were not very good, and no one was fooled. Britain punished Boston with harsh laws that made the colonists angrier than ever.

In September of 1774 men from every colony except Georgia met in Philadelphia to talk about protecting the colonists' interests, which no longer seemed to many to be the same as Great Britain's interests. They agreed

Bostonians cheer as Samuel Adams and other Patriots, disguised as Native Americans, throw British tea into Boston Harbor. Similar "tea parties" occurred in New York and Annapolis, Maryland.

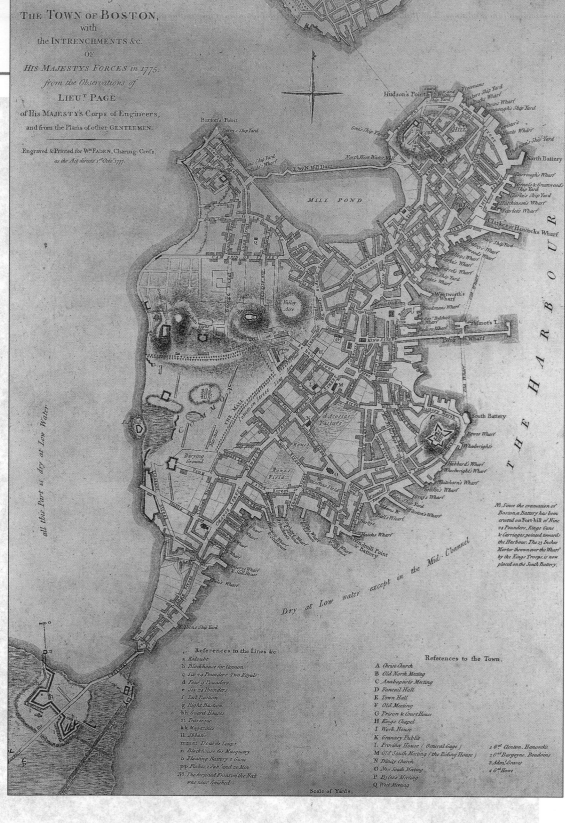

By 1775, when a British officer made this map of Boston, tension between colonists and British troops in the city was high. The map shows British artillery and marines stationed in the open area known as the Common, ready to quell any public violence that might erupt.

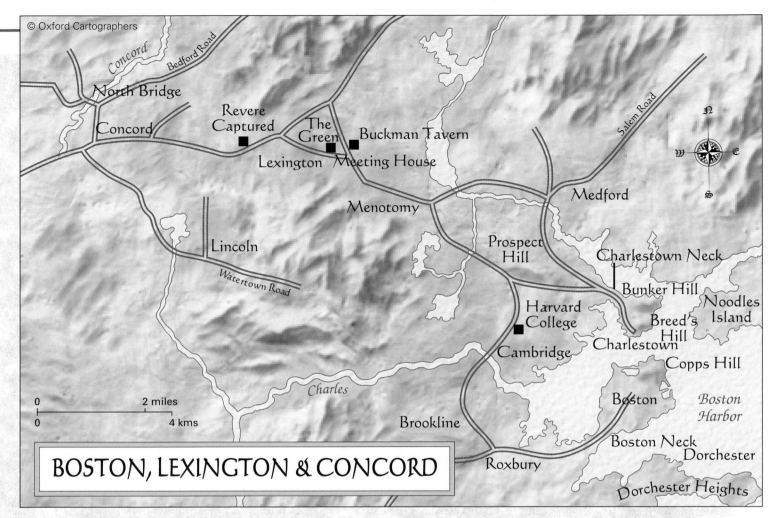

BOSTON, LEXINGTON & CONCORD

During the night of April 18, 1775, a Boston doctor out for a stroll saw British troops marching out of the Common. He alerted Paul Revere, a noted Patriot, who rode out of Boston and through the nearby town of Lexington, shouting along the way the news that British soldiers were on the move, no doubt headed for the supply of Patriot weapons at Concord. The British captured Revere before he reached Concord, but the Patriots received enough warning to get most of their precious gunpowder out of the storehouse in Concord. Armed with the long rifles they used for hunting ducks, Patriots lined the roads and fired steadily on the redcoats as they marched back from Concord to Boston.

to form militias, companies of citizen soldiers prepared to fight in an emergency. War, it seemed, might be just around the corner. A British officer in Boston wrote that the colonists were "taking every means to provide themselves with arms."

The Road to War

General Thomas L. Gage, the commander of the British army in North America, decided to put troops on Bunker Hill and Breed's Hill north of Boston harbor. From there they could control Boston, firing cannon on it if necessary. But word leaked out about Gage's plans, and the militiamen beat him to the hills. When Gage's troops stormed the hills on June 17, the militia

Red-coated British troops force the colonial militia to retreat from the Battle of Bunker Hill. The British won the battle, but their victory cost them many men. After Bunker Hill a member of the British government said gloomily that it would be "no easy matter to tame such fighters [as the colonists]."

drove them back twice with **musket** fire. Finally, tired and low on ammunition, the militia **retreated** and Gage's men took the hills.

The British won the Battle of Bunker Hill, but at a cost. More than 1,000 of Gage's men—nearly half his force—were killed or wounded. A British officer wrote that "another such [victory] would have ruined us." Now the British knew that the colonists were a real threat. And the colonists began to be divided into Patriots, who supported the rebellion, and Loyalists, who remained loyal to Great Britain.

Lexington, Concord, and Bunker Hill

By 1775 more than 3,000 British soldiers were stationed around Boston. On April 19 a party of them went to capture a **stockpile** of militia weapons in the nearby town of Concord. A local militia attacked the redcoats at Lexington, on the way to Concord, and all along the road from Concord back to Boston. They killed 73 redcoats and wounded 200 others. The British could not let them get away with it.

Americans Declare Independence

Up to this point the Patriots had not been fighting for independence. Some of them, such as the **agitator** Patrick Henry and writer

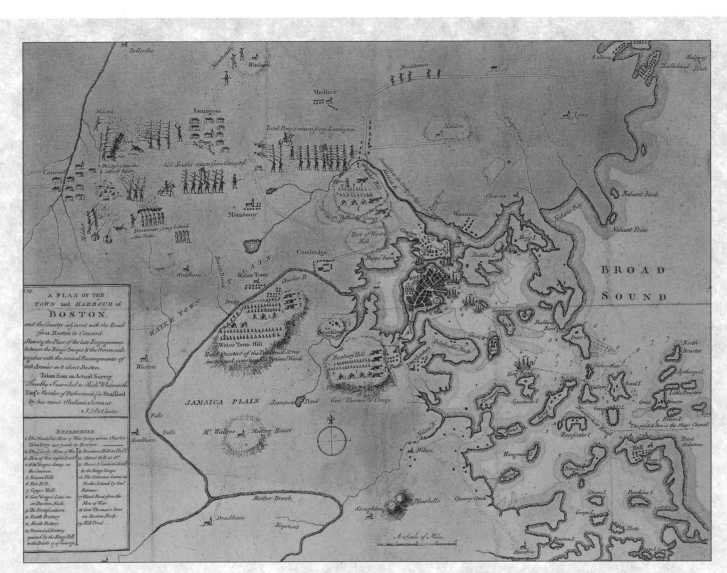

A British "Officer on the Spot" drew this plan of the Battle of Bunker Hill. The dotted lines show the three ships that ferried redcoats from Boston Harbor to the foot of the hill, where the Americans fired down on them. The Americans had so little ammunition, however, that their leader, Colonel William Prescott, told his men, "Don't fire until you see the whites of their eyes, boys." Prescott didn't want the militia to waste ammunition on long-range shots that would probably miss their targets. Despite this precaution, the Americans could not stop the British advance and finally had to retreat.

THE PATRIOTS CHOOSE A COMMANDER

 In May of 1775 Patriot leaders met again in Philadelphia. This time even Georgia, which had many colonists loyal to Britain, sent a representative. The congress agreed that although each colony would maintain its own militia, the Americans needed a unified military force. They created the Continental Army, and to command it, they chose George Washington, who had gained much militia experience during the French and Indian War. Tall, impressive on horseback, responsible toward his duties, Washington won the admiration and loyalty of many soldiers who served under him. George Washington was also from the south. Because the fighting had all been in New England, it would have been easy for the southern colonies to ignore the rebellion. By choosing a Virginian as their commander, however, the Patriot leaders encouraged the southern colonists to think of it as their fight, too.

George Washington, a Virginia planter and an experienced soldier, was the first commander-in-chief of the Continental Army. In addition to providing military leadership, Washington spoke out strongly for complete independence from Great Britain. Patriots admired him so much that some wanted to make him king of America.

Thomas Paine, *did* want the colonies to make a complete break from Great Britain. In the early summer of 1776 they would ask Thomas Jefferson of Virginia to write a Declaration of Independence.

Other Patriots, however, hoped that the relationship between the parent country and the colonies could be mended. They wrote to King George III of Great Britain, offering to make a deal. The colonists would stop fighting if the British government met their demands for lower taxes and less meddling in colonial government. Instead of listening to the offer, the king sent 500 ships, 10,000 sailors, and 32,000 soldiers to New York in the summer of 1776. A forest of tents sprang up on Staten Island to house the soldiers. Great Britain, it seemed, meant to teach its rebellious colonies a stern lesson.

On July 4, less than a week after the first British troop ships arrived, the Patriot leaders in Philadelphia voted in favor of Jefferson's Declaration. The fighting was no longer an uprising against unfair laws. It had become an all-out war for independence.

Representatives sign the Declaration of Independence at the Second Continental Congress.
The Philadelphia building where they met is now a national landmark called Independence Hall.

Chapter Two

THE WAR IN
THE NORTH

Fighting between the British and the Americans continued for a year between Bunker Hill and the Declaration of Independence. Washington and his officers and men carried on with the war in the northern colonies. Each side won important victories and suffered bitter defeats.

The Northern Frontier

Even before the Battle of Bunker Hill the Patriots won a northern victory. A group of men from the Green Mountains of northern New England, led by Ethan Allen, had captured a British outpost called Fort Ticonderoga that lay along the route between New York and Canada. Two columns of Patriot troops then attacked the British in Canada. One group marched north from Ticonderoga and, after a **siege** of two months, captured the fort that protected the city of Montreal.

An officer named Benedict Arnold led the other attack on Canada, approaching Quebec through what is now Maine. His men struggled to row up fast-flowing rivers and marched during a cold, wet autumn through what one soldier called "hideous woods and ravines." All their effort was for nothing. They failed to take Quebec and had to retreat in the spring. By June of 1776 all colonial troops had left Canada, which played little part in the rest of the war. Benedict Arnold, though, would appear again. A few years later the British paid him

WAR IN THE NORTH 1776-1778

Lake Huron

Lake Ontario

Fort O

Lake Erie

C

Fort Pitt

Clark

Ohio

Proclamation line 1763

PE

Potoma

M

VIRGINIA

© Oxford Cartographers

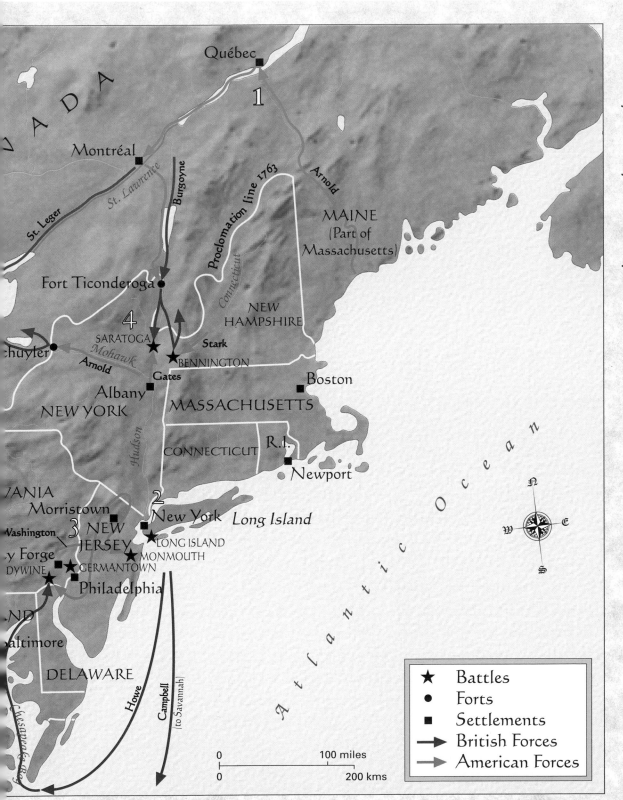

Québec

1

Montréal

St. Lawrence

St. Leger

Burgoyne

Arnold

Proclamation line 1763

MAINE
(Part of
Massachusetts)

Fort Ticonderoga

NEW
HAMPSHIRE

Connecticut

4

SARATOGA

Stark

Schuyler

Mohawk

BENNINGTON

Arnold

Gates

Boston

Albany

NEW YORK

MASSACHUSETTS

Hudson

CONNECTICUT

R.I.

Newport

Morristown

2

New York

Long Island

Washington

3

NEW
JERSEY

LONG ISLAND

y Forge

MONMOUTH

DYWINE

GERMANTOWN

Philadelphia

DELAWARE

Howe

Campbell
(to Savannah)

A t l a n t i c   O c e a n

N

W   E

S

★ Battles

● Forts

■ Settlements

➡ British Forces

➡ American Forces

0   100 miles
0   200 kms

During the first years of the American Revolution, most fighting took place in the north. The fortunes of war seesawed, with first one side and then the other gaining the upper hand. The Americans tried and failed to take Canada, while the British tried and failed to drive a wedge between New England and other states.

1. The Americans invade Canada.
2. The Battle of Long Island.
3. The Americans retreat to New Jersey. The British capture Philadelphia.
4. The Americans defeat the British in Saratoga.
5. George Rogers Clark attacks British outposts in the Ohio Valley.

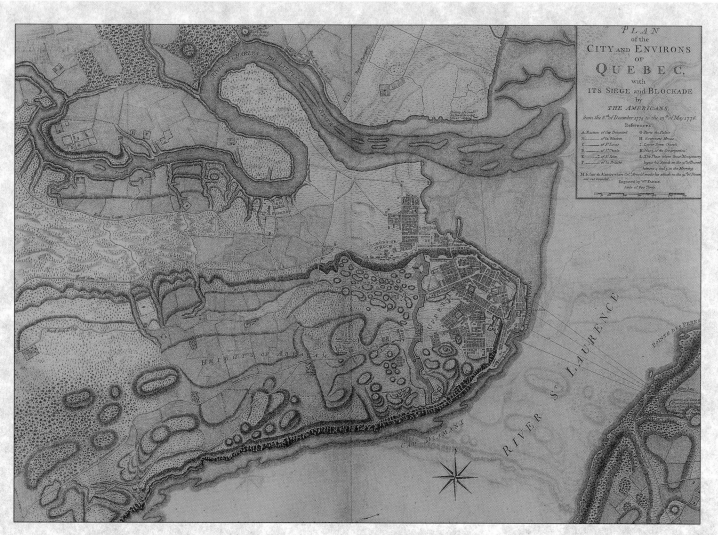

PLAN
of the
CITY AND ENVIRONS
OF
QUEBEC,
with
ITS SIEGE and BLOCKADE
by
THE AMERICANS.
from the 8th of December 1775 to the 13th of May 1776.

The British in Canada believed that the Upper City of Quebec, perched on a clifftop and surrounded by a fortified wall, was unconquerable—even though they had captured it from the French during the Seven Years' War, just a few years earlier. American forces led by Colonel Benedict Arnold tried throughout one long, miserably cold winter to capture the city. They fired on it from across the river and from outside its western wall, but in the end they had to give up and withdraw southward. During the attack British forces in Quebec killed Richard Montgomery, an American general, and took many prisoners, most of whom were later returned to the colonies.

to change sides. When the Americans learned of Arnold's betrayal, the traitor fled to London, where he would spend the rest of his life.

The British Strike Back

A bit farther south, Washington drove the British out of Boston in March of 1776—but the British promptly focused their attention on New York. If they could take and hold New York, they would drive a red-coated wedge into the heart of the American colonies. Washington moved his headquarters to New York, determined to defend it. Unfortunately for Washington, the Continental Army met defeat in battles on Long Island and along the Hudson River. Step by step the British drove Washington and his men back, forcing them to retreat south into New Jersey and then Pennsylvania. But on Christmas night, 1776, Washington silently crossed the Delaware River and attacked the enemy at Trenton, New Jersey, catching the groggy soldiers off guard. It was a much-needed victory for the hard-pressed Continentals.

The war went much the same way in 1777—success for the British, followed by important victories for the Americans. In September a British force captured Philadelphia, the closest thing to an American capital. But the British had a serious problem. Their generals in America made battle plans that had to be approved by the king and his advisors. Because

Plunging into a creek, American troops retreat from the advancing British in the Battle of Long Island, which ended in an American defeat. Long Island saw another Patriot tragedy when the British hanged a Connecticut schoolteacher named Nathan Hale, whom they had caught spying on their troops. Tradition says that Hale's patriotic last words were, "I only regret that I have but one life to lose for my country."

it took months for communications to cross the ocean and replies to return, British plans could easily fall apart. That's what happened to their complex plan to seize New York's Hudson River valley and cut New England off from the rest of the colonies. The three British armies that were supposed to work together did not cooperate. The first army remained in Philadelphia instead of marching north to help the other two, which ran into trouble in northern New York.

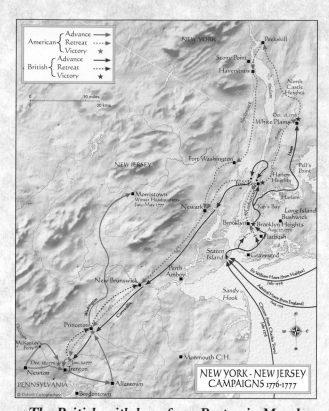

Legend (map):
American — Advance, Retreat, Victory ★
British — Advance, Retreat, Victory ★

NEW YORK — NEW JERSEY CAMPAIGNS 1776-1777

© Oxford Cartographers

The British withdrew from Boston in March 1776. From then to January 1777, the most important scenes of combat were in New York and New Jersey. The British wanted to control this region so that they could isolate New England and keep the American forces from acting with unity. They inflicted a stinging defeat on the Americans in the Battle of Long Island, where more than one British officer remarked on the poor equipment and skimpy supplies of the Continentals. Washington withdrew his army into Manhattan. The British pursued. He withdrew again and again, first north along the Hudson River and then south through New Jersey, with the British following every step of the way. The year ended, however, with several American victories at Trenton. These successes did not gain much in the way of military advantages, but they lifted the sagging spirits of the cold, weary, and hungry Continental soldiers in their winter camp.

Continentals halted the second British force at Fort Stanwix and defeated the third at Saratoga.

Into the West

In spite of the Proclamation of 1763, colonists had already begun carving out settlements west of the boundary line. Daniel Boone, for example, had led an early party of settlers into Kentucky, and by the mid-1770s about 10,000 Americans were living in what was supposed to be Indian land west of the Appalachians. The war soon spread into this western territory.

Native Americans who had sided with the French against the British just a few years earlier now decided to side with the British against the Americans. The British had at least *tried* to keep settlers out of Indian country, but the American settlers kept pushing. They gave no sign that they would respect Indian claims. Some Indians saw the Revolutionary War as their chance to choose the lesser of two evils.

George Rogers Clark, a colonel in the Virginia militia, led the American forces on the western frontier. His opponent was Henry Hamilton, the British commander at Fort Detroit. Americans called him "Hamilton the hair buyer" because of rumors that he paid Indians for settlers' scalps. By capturing key British posts at Kaskaskia, Cahokia, and Vincennes—he captured Vincennes twice, in fact—Clark kept the British and their Indian allies from ruling the western frontier. Fighting would

WINNING ALLIES

When news of the American victory at Saratoga reached the other side of the Atlantic, it angered and embarrassed the British, but it made Britain's enemies take a second look at what was happening in North America. Patriot Benjamin Franklin had been in France for months, trying to get Britain's old enemy to enter the war openly on the American side. Once the French saw that the Americans might actually *win* the war, they joined the effort and sent aid in the form of money, supplies, ships, and men. Spain and the Netherlands also attacked Great Britain, not because they liked the Americans but because they hated Britain. Franklin and the Patriots didn't care *why* their allies gave support. They would take any help they could get.

Benjamin Franklin was a hero of the Revolution, but not for fighting. He spent the revolutionary years in Paris persuading the French to join the war as allies of the Americans.

continue there, however. In fact, the last battle of the American Revolution would take place at Blue Licks, Kentucky, in August of 1782, long after fighting had stopped in the coastal colonies.

War at Sea

While armies maneuvered across the North American landscape, ships and sailors fought a wider-ranging war at sea. The Patriots had managed to scrape together an army, but they didn't have a navy. They did have privateers—privately owned ships whose captains, each acting independently, would attack British navy and commercial vessels. During the early years of the war, the sea fighting was between these American privateers and British ships.

General Sir William Howe, the British commander, launched the 1777 campaign by shipping his army from New York to the head of Chesapeake Bay and marching north to Philadelphia. The British surrounded the city on the north and west. The Americans, under Washington, tried to stop them at Brandywine Creek and again at Germantown but failed both times. As the British marched into Philadelphia in September of 1777, the Patriot members of the Continental Congress fled the city, hiding out in the country to avoid capture. Howe was pleased with himself for taking "the rebels' capital," but by focusing on Philadelphia he failed to carry out his part in a complex British campaign in northern New York. His absence may have contributed to British defeats there.

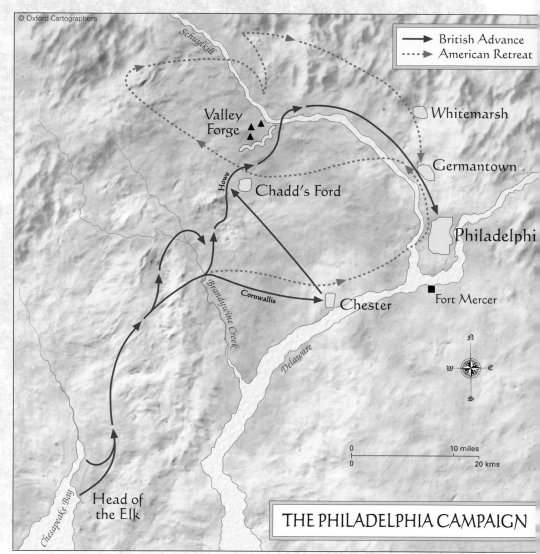

THE PHILADELPHIA CAMPAIGN

After France joined the war on the American side, however, a French fleet came to the Patriots' aid. The British navy had to block American ports so that the Patriots could not receive supplies, to protect British supply ships, and to move troops around. It also had to protect Barbados and Britain's other West Indian island colonies in the Caribbean Sea. But the French had their own West Indian colonies where they could muster ships and

At the time of its capture by the British, Philadelphia was the third-largest city in the colonies, after Boston and New York. The labeled buildings sprinkled across the countryside represent individual farms, while the picture at the bottom of the map is of the building now called Independence Hall.

The Virginia legislature sent George Rogers Clark and a company of volunteers against the British outposts in the Ohio River valley. Clark's men took Kaskaskia, Great Britain's main outpost in Illinois, on July 4, 1778, exactly two years after the Declaration of Independence had been proclaimed in Philadelphia. He then captured Cahokia and Vincennes. Henry Hamilton, the British commander in the region, recaptured Vincennes, so Clark took it again in early 1779. Clark's swashbuckling victories not only quieted unrest among the British and the Indians on the western frontier but also gave the Americans a claim to the Ohio River country a few years later, when they sat down to talk peace terms with Great Britain.

WAR IN THE WEST 1778-1779

★ Battles
● Forts
→ British Forces
→ American Forces

© Oxford Cartographers

troops. While the British were trying to fight the Patriots in North America, they also had to fight a series of naval battles in the West Indies. France and Great Britain attacked each other's islands again and again. France won control of a British island called St. Kitts and came close to seizing Jamaica. These sea battles helped the Patriot cause by draining some of Britain's strength away from the fighting in North America. Ships patrolling the Carib-

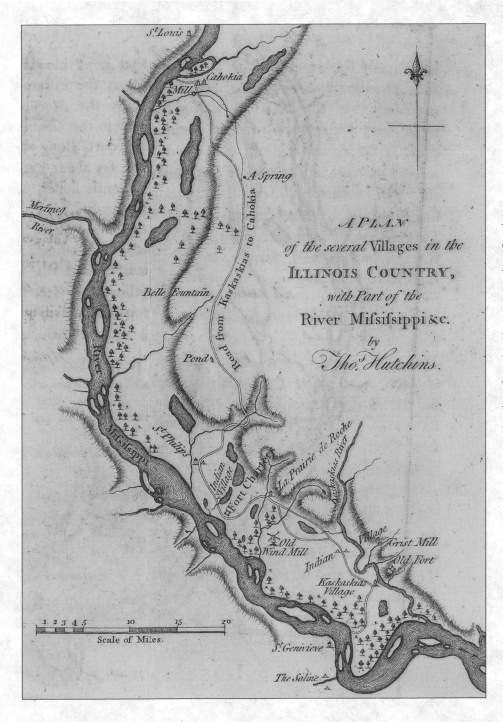

A PLAN

of the several Villages *in the*

ILLINOIS COUNTRY,

with Part of the

River Mifsifsippi &c.

by

Tho.ˢ Hutchins.

Scale of Miles.

This 1778 map shows the British settlements at Kaskaskia and Cahokia, in Illinois. French names such as "La Prairie" and "Fort Chartres," however, are reminders that the French were exploring and trading along the upper Mississippi River long before the British came on the scene.

A VICTORY IN BRITISH WATERS

 The most remarkable triumph of an American privateer in the Revolutionary War took place not in American waters but close to the coast of Great Britain. In September of 1779 John Paul Jones, captain of the *Bonhomme Richard*, attacked the much larger British warship *Serapis*. After a desperate three-hour battle, in which the ships were locked close together, pounding each other with cannonballs, the *Serapis* surrendered—and the Patriots had another hero.

The American privateer John Paul Jones, sailing an old French vessel that Benjamin Franklin had gotten for him, captures the larger British ship Serapis *in what a French naval officer called "the most gallant act of this noble war."*

bean could not be used to **blockade** American harbors.

The Northern War Winds Down

By spring of 1778 the war in the north had become something of a standoff. The British were leaving Philadelphia because their commanders feared that they might be cut off there, unable to receive supplies. But they still held New York firmly, although they were unable to gain much ground elsewhere. On the other hand, Washington's Continental Army was not strong enough to take New York, although the general directed raids on other British outposts in New Jersey.

Washington also struck back against some of the Native American groups who had sided with the British in the Ohio River valley and elsewhere. Some of the most vicious fighting of the war occurred in frontier **skirmishes** between the British and Indians on one side and the American settlers, militia, and soldiers on the other. Both sides were guilty of acts of horrible violence and cruelty. Washington told General John Sullivan of New Hampshire to crush the Iroquois Confederacy, a group of six tribes that had raided settlements in northern and western New York and Pennsylvania. He defeated them in a major battle near the Pennsylvania-New York border in 1779, but fighting continued on the bloody New York frontier for two more years.

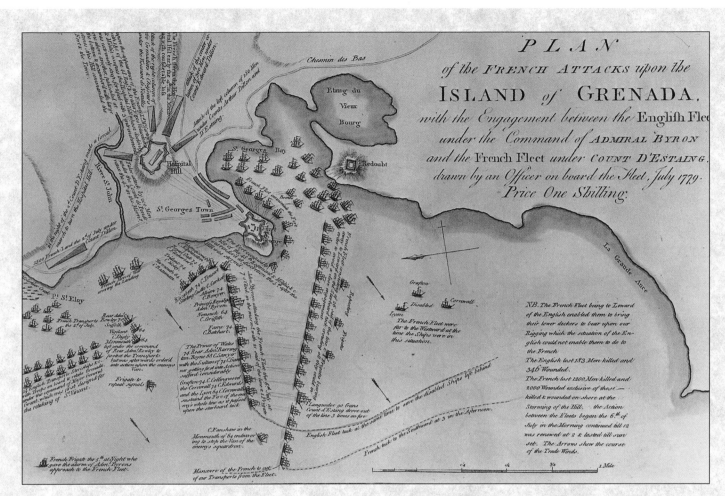

The American Revolution was also fought outside the present borders of the United States. Great Britain had colonies on islands in the West Indies, south of Florida, and they, too, became involved in the fighting. After France entered the war on the side of the Americans, French fleets attacked British island colonies. This British map from 1779 shows French ships attacking Grenada, an island where the British operated many valuable sugarcane plantations. A note on the map explains that the French ships were able to fire their guns into the sails and rigging of the British ships, which were pinned against the shore. The French had the upper hand in this fight until another British fleet approached and frightened them off.

Chapter Three

THE WAR IN
THE SOUTH

aval fighting continued until the end of the Revolutionary War, but the land war took a new direction in late 1778, when the British turned their focus southward. They hoped that the presence of many Loyalists in the south would give them an advantage. The war that had begun in Massachusetts would be settled by battles in Georgia, the Carolinas, and Virginia.

General Charles Cornwallis in 1805, more than twenty years after the siege of Yorktown. Cornwallis's defeat in America didn't hurt his standing in Britain—after the Revolution he held the important post of governor-general of India, Britain's most valuable colony.

Striking at Southern Ports

In 1778 the British launched their new **campaign**. Their plan was to combine sea and land power in an attack on two major southern ports: Savannah, in Georgia, and Charleston, in South Carolina.

The attack on Savannah took place in November of 1778 and was a huge success for the British, who easily captured the city. The lieutenant who led the British attackers boasted, "I may venture to say, Sir, that I have ripped one star and one stripe from the Rebel flag of America." The following year the Americans and an allied French fleet made a determined effort to recapture Savannah. They failed— and lost many men in the attempt.

Georgia was in British hands, but still worse was ahead for the Americans. In February of 1780 an army of 8,000 redcoats and a naval fleet laid siege to Charleston, surrounding the city by land and sea and firing upon it. An American officer later said, "It appeared as if the stars were tumbling down...cannon balls whizzing and shells hissing continually... ammunition chests blowing up, great guns bursting and wounded men groaning." After several months the city surrendered. The British captured 5,000 prisoners. Soon after their victory, the British commander, General Henry Clinton, sailed off to New York, leaving General Charles Cornwallis in charge of Charleston. In Great Britain a member of the gov-

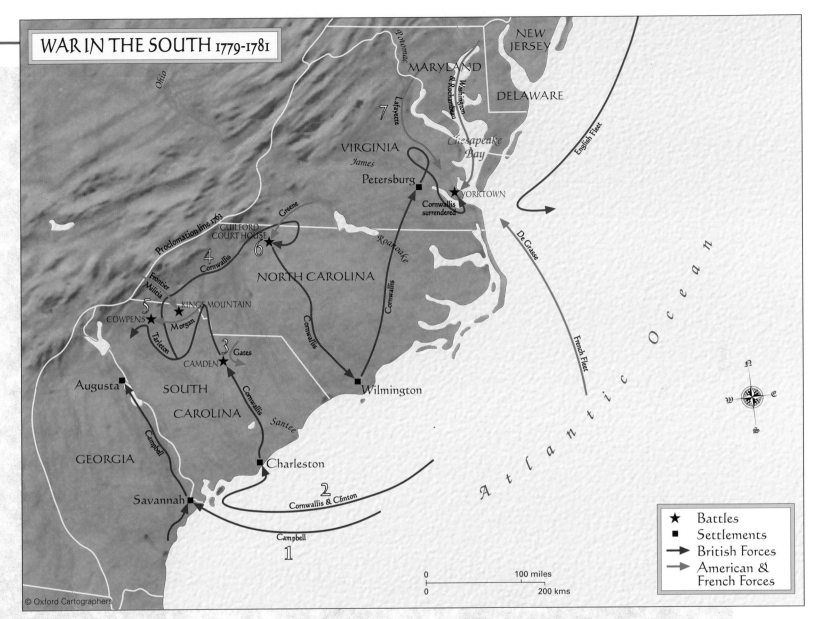

WAR IN THE SOUTH 1779-1781

NEW JERSEY

MARYLAND

DELAWARE

Ohio

Potomac

Lafayette

7

Washington & Rochambeau

Chesapeake Bay

VIRGINIA

James

English Fleet

Petersburg

Cornwallis surrendered

YORKTOWN

Greene

Proclamation line 1763

GUILFORD COURT HOUSE

6

De Grasse

4

Cornwallis

NORTH CAROLINA

Roanoke

Frontier Militia

KINGS MOUNTAIN

Cornwallis

French Fleet

5

COWPENS

Morgan

Tarleton

3

Gates

Cornwallis

CAMDEN

Augusta

SOUTH CAROLINA

Santee

Wilmington

Campbell

GEORGIA

Cornwallis

Charleston

2

Cornwallis & Clinton

Savannah

Campbell

1

A t l a n t i c   O c e a n

0   100 miles
0   200 kms

★ Battles
■ Settlements
→ British Forces
→ American & French Forces

© Oxford Cartographers

The most significant battles of the second half of the Revolutionary War took place in the south. The principal British commanders were Generals Henry Clinton and Charles Cornwallis. Their opponents included not only George Washington and the Continental Army but also a French war fleet and a number of wily Americans who had mastered the art of fighting in a challenging landscape.

1. *The British attack Savannah, 1778.*
2. *The British siege of Charleston, 1780.*
3. *General Cornwallis defeats the Americans in Camden.*
4. *The British march invade North Carolina.*
5. *American victory in the battle of Kings Mountain and Cowpens.*
6. *British victory at Guilford Courthouse.*
7. *The American and French troops march to Yorktown.*

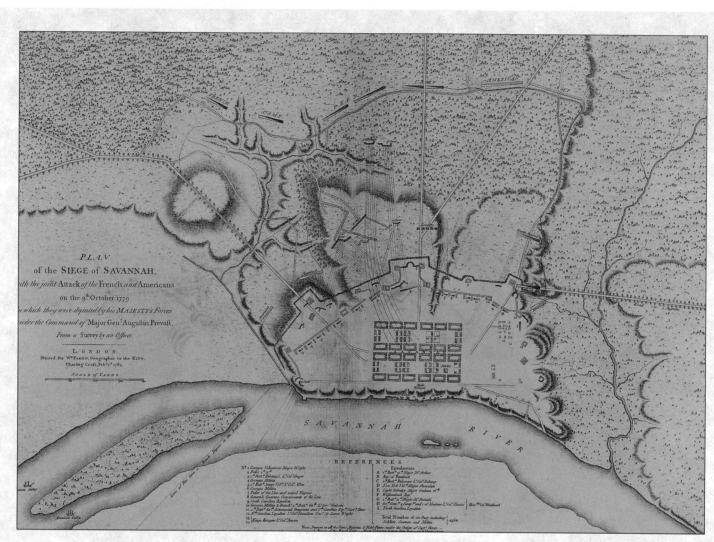

In 1784, after the Revolution had ended and the British had reluctantly recognized the independence of their former colonies, William Faden, the official mapmaker to the British crown, drew this plan of the American and French siege of Savannah in 1779. The caption proudly boasts that the attackers "were defeated by his MAJESTY's forces." Victories in Savannah and Charleston gave new hope to the British, but that hope did not last long. British forces could hold the ports but could not control rebellion in the countryside.

ernment declared happily that America was all but beaten.

Guerrilla Warfare

Georgia and South Carolina had fallen to the British, but, even with the support of local Loyalists, the redcoats could not keep the peace. There were Patriots in the south as well as Loyalists, and some of them became big nuisances to the British.

The British troops fought in the traditional European style. They marched in large groups, often to music, and they expected to meet the enemy face-to-face on a battlefield. But Patriots in the south now challenged the British with a different kind of warfare—lightning-fast, hit-and-run raids by sneaky, swift-moving groups. This kind of fighting is now called guerrilla warfare, and several South Carolina Patriots proved very good at it.

After the British burned his plantation, Andrew Pickens formed a guerrilla band and led hundreds of raids. Francis Marion used his knowledge of South Carolina's wilderness and of Indian survival methods to become "the Swamp Fox," a raider whom the British could never catch because he and his men hid out in muddy, mosquito-infested swamps between their attacks on British wagon trains and patrols. The guerrilla raiders made it impossible for the British to control the countryside and kept them penned in the big coastal ports.

Cornwallis Moves North

Cornwallis set out to invade North Carolina in the fall of 1780. He turned back after learning that Patriot riflemen had wiped out 1,000 Loyalists in a battle at Kings Mountain, along his line of march. Cornwallis did, however, manage to invade North Carolina in early 1781. He won a battle against the Continentals at Guilford Courthouse in central North Carolina, but his losses were heavy. He withdrew to the coast and then moved north into Virginia.

Some historians say that Cornwallis was retreating from the south. Others claim that he had been planning an attack on Virginia. Either way, he marched deeper and deeper into Virginia, attacking Patriot strongholds along the way. At Yorktown, a port on the Virginia coast, he settled into a well-protected camp. A Patriot force besieged Yorktown on the land side, but Cornwallis expected the British navy to bring him more men and supplies.

Siege of Yorktown

Washington had been planning to attack the British army in New York. But, with Cornwallis holed up in Yorktown, he changed his plan. Under Washington's orders, a French fleet hurried to Yorktown to cut the British off from escape or aid by sea. At the same time, American and French troops closed in on the city by land. Soon Cornwallis's 8,000 men were surrounded by 17,000 of their enemies.

THOMAS JEFFERSON'S CLOSE CALL

 As the British troops under Cornwallis marched through Virginia, they set fire to Richmond, the capital. Led by Governor Thomas Jefferson, the state government fled to Charlottesville. Soon afterward Jefferson retired from the governorship and returned to his home. Then he learned that British troops were close at hand, perhaps on their way to capture him. Jefferson fled into the Virginia hills and managed to escape the British. Later some people accused him of failing to protect the capital and of being a coward. The Virginia government investigated these charges and declared that Jefferson had acted rightly. After all, it would have hurt the American cause if the British had captured the author of the Declaration of Independence!

Thomas Jefferson, author of the Declaration of Independence. Some Patriots, including George Washington, criticized Jefferson for not bearing arms during the fight for independence. Jefferson, however, believed that he could make a better contribution as a writer, lawmaker, and governor of Virginia than as a soldier.

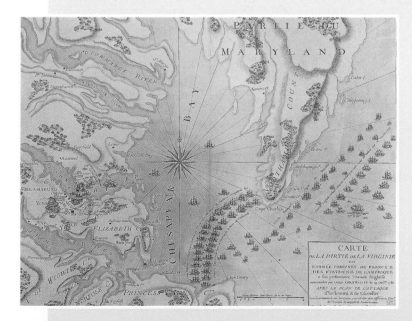

The Virginia port of Yorktown on the Chesapeake Bay. To this day no one knows why General Cornwallis left North Carolina to march through Virginia, or why he allowed himself to be trapped in Yorktown. General Clinton, his superior officer, later accused Cornwallis of having disobeyed instructions—and possibly of having lost the war for Great Britain.

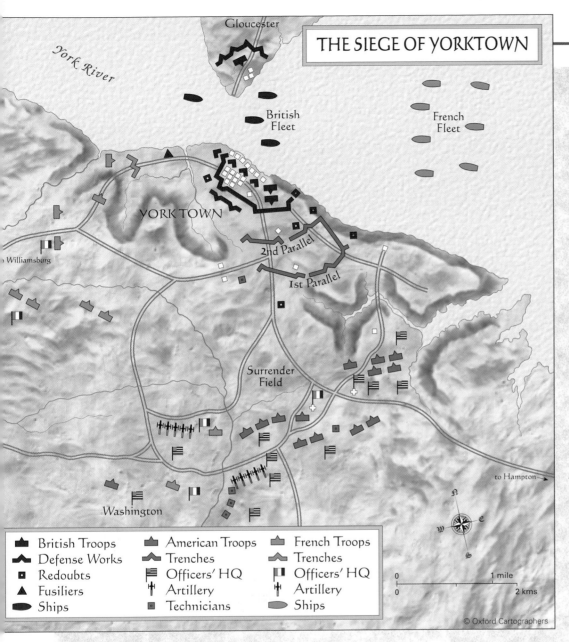

THE SIEGE OF YORKTOWN

Gloucester

York River

British Fleet

French Fleet

YORK TOWN

to Williamsburg

2nd Parallel

1st Parallel

Surrender Field

to Hampton

Washington

British Troops	**American Troops**	**French Troops**
Defense Works	Trenches	Trenches
Redoubts	Officers' HQ	Officers' HQ
Fusiliers	Artillery	Artillery
Ships	Technicians	Ships

0   1 mile
0   2 kms

© Oxford Cartographers

The Patriots' French allies played a key part in the siege of Yorktown, as well as in other American victories that won the war in the south. The British forces could defend Yorktown—but they could not get out, and they could not obtain food, ammunition, or other supplies. French and American soldiers ringed the city by land, and by sea a French fleet blocked the entrance to the harbor. The place marked "Surrender Field" is where Cornwallis formally surrendered, handing his sword to General Washington. As was the custom, Washington politely returned it in a gesture of respect for the dignity of the defeated commander.

Then, on October 11, 1781, the bombing began. Guns fired on Yorktown day and night. The British were running out of food and lacked medical care for their wounded. On October 19 Cornwallis surrendered to Washington.

The Battle of Yorktown was the real end of the Revolutionary War, although some fighting on land and sea continued for another year. But Yorktown convinced the British that the cost of the war was too high, and they agreed to

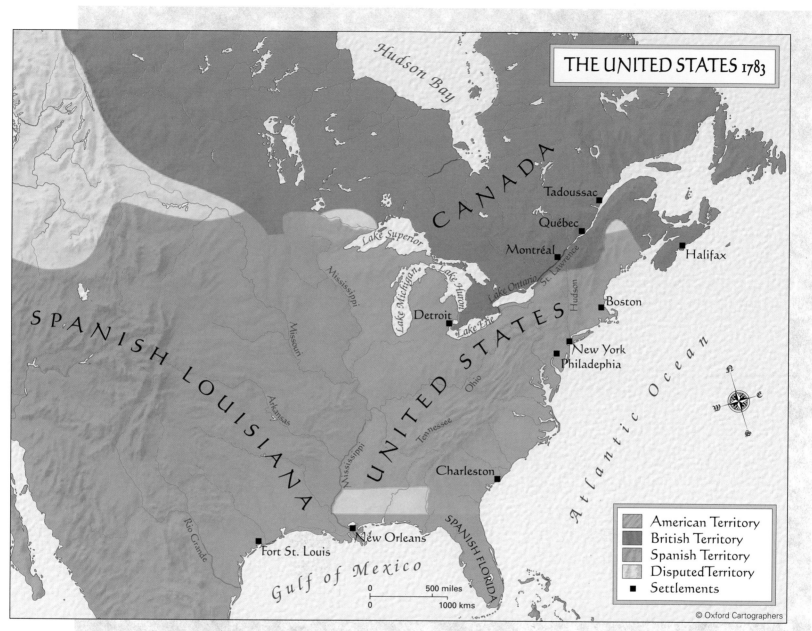

THE UNITED STATES 1783

Hudson Bay

CANADA

Tadoussac

Québec

Montréal

Halifax

Lake Superior

Mississippi

Lake Michigan

Lake Huron

Lake Ontario

St. Lawrence

Boston

SPANISH LOUISIANA

Missouri

Detroit

Lake Erie

UNITED STATES

Hudson

New York
Philadephia

Atlantic Ocean

Arkansas

Ohio

Tennessee

Mississippi

Charleston

Rio Grande

New Orleans

Fort St. Louis

SPANISH FLORIDA

Gulf of Mexico

0   500 miles
0   1000 kms

	American Territory
	British Territory
	Spanish Territory
	Disputed Territory
■	Settlements

© Oxford Cartographers

*Just as in 1763, at the end of the Seven Years' War, the map of North America was redrawn in
1783, as territory again changed hands at the peace table after a long and bitter conflict.
This time, however, the map recorded the birth of a new nation, the United States.*

give the colonies their independence. Men from America and Great Britain met in France in early 1782 to work out the terms of peace. They signed the final agreement, known as the Treaty of Paris, on September 3, 1783.

The New Nation

The Treaty of Paris was the birth certificate of a new nation, the United States of America. Great Britain recognized that country's independence and its new borders. The British got to keep Canada, but they had to remove their troops from American territory, which stretched from Canada to Spanish Florida and from the Atlantic coast to the Mississippi River.

One sore point at the treaty talks was the fate of the Loyalists. During the Revolutionary War, many had fled to Canada, where they would remain. But many others had stayed in the colonies, sometimes fighting on the British side. Patriots had robbed, harassed, and attacked them. Under the Treaty, the new American government promised to return the property it had seized from Loyalists, but it returned very little.

A big job faced the leaders and people of the new nation. They had to heal the wounds between Patriots and Loyalists and build a sense of American unity. They had to earn a place in the world community of nations. And they had to decide what to do about the Native Americans and the western frontier. But now, after the Revolutionary War, they were free to make those decisions for themselves.

Cornwallis and his officers march out of Yorktown after surrendering to Washington. As they marched, the British military band played an old children's song called "The World Turned Upside Down." For the British, the mighty power that had once ruled North America, the tune was the simple truth.

Glossary

agitator: One who stirs up, or agitates, public opinion.

blockade: Using ships to block the entrance to a harbor or port, which keeps the city from selling or receiving goods.

campaign: A planned action or series of actions to achieve a particular goal or result.

frontier: A place where settled territory meets wilderness.

musket: A long-barreled gun that fired lead balls; accurate at distances of about 75 yards (69 meters).

plantation agriculture: A system of farming in which a single crop is grown over a large area and sold for export rather than being used locally.

retreat: To withdraw from or leave the scene of combat.

siege: A military operation in which an attacking force surrounds a fort or city, cutting it off from supplies and reinforcements.

skirmish: A minor fight in a war compared to larger battles.

stockpile: A storehouse or reserve supply.

Map List

ABOUT THE HISTORICAL MAPS

The historical maps used in this book are primary source documents found in The Library of Congress Map Division. You can find these maps on pages 11, 14, 17, 24, 29, 31, 33, 38, and 40.

Chronology

1763   Great Britain wins control of eastern North America and tries to keep settlers from crossing Appalachian Mountains.

1770   Boston Massacre highlights tension between American colonists and Great Britain.

1773   Colonists protest British taxes with a "Tea Party" in Boston harbor.

1775   First shots of war fired at Concord and Lexington; Battle of Bunker Hill.

1776   Americans declare their independence from Great Britain on July 4.

1777   British capture American capital, Philadelphia.

1778–1779   George Rogers Clark battles British and Indians on northwest frontier.

1779   John Paul Jones defeats the British warship *Serapis.*

1780   War shifts to South, with fighting in Carolinas.

1781   War ends after Americans defeat British at Yorktown, Virginia.

1783   Treaty of Paris officially establishes independence of the United States of America.

Further Reading

Carter, Alden. *At the Forge of Liberty.* New York: Franklin Watts, 1988.

Collier, Christopher and James L. Collier. *The American Revolution, 1763–1783.* New York: Benchmark Books, 1998.

Marrin, Albert. *The War for Independence: The Story of the American Revolution.* New York: Atheneum, 1988.

Meltzer, Milton, editor. *The American Revolutionaries: A History in Their Own Words.* New York: Crowell, 1987.

Morris, Robert. *The American Revolution.* Minneapolis: Lerner Publications, 1985.

Wilbur, C. Keith. *The Revolutionary Soldier.* New York: Chelsea House, 1993.

WEBSITES

The Library of Congress Geography
and Maps: An Illustrated Guide
www.loc.gov/rr/geogmap/guide

Map History
www.maphist.nl

Map Societies
www.csuohio.edu/CUT/MapSoc/Name_indx.htm

ABOUT THE AUTHOR

Rebecca Stefoff has published more than 50 books for young readers, including many volumes on the exploration, settlement, and history of North America. She now makes her home in Portland, Oregon, but formerly she lived just a few blocks from Independence Hall in Philadelphia and often visited Valley Forge and other important sites of the American Revolution.

Index

Entries are filed letter-by-letter. Page numbers for illustrations and maps are in boldface.